Real Estate Development

For People in a Hurry

By: J.H. De la Maza

"Make no little plans. They have no magic to stir men's blood and probably will not themselves be realized. Make big plans, aim high in hope and work, remembering that a noble, logical diagram once recorded will never die, but long after we are gone will be a living thing, asserting itself with ever growing insistency. Remember that our sons and grandsons are going to do things that would stagger us."

- *Daniel Burnham*

Real Estate Development

For People in a Hurry

To my wife, family, and friends. You guys make life worth living.

Table of Contents

Preface: 1

Chapter 1: Know the Players 4

Chapter 2: Architecture; The Artists 7

Chapter 3: Investments; The Dreamers 13

Chapter 4: Joint Ventures & Waterfalls; Dealmakers 25

Chapter 5: Pre-Construction; The Detectives. 30

Chapter 6: Design Management; The Boundaries 48

Chapter 7: Construction Management;
Boots on the Ground 55

Chapter 8: General Contractors; The Builders 67

Chapter 9: Property Managers & Leases; The Salesman ... 75

Chapter 10: Thinking Forward 80

Preface:

People rarely think about what a building or real estate is and what it represents. If we start thinking about it in detail, we will realize that it can mean a plethora of things to various individuals, and all can be true at the same time. Professionals in finance would say that buildings are to be viewed as assets that generate cash flow, an investor might say that buildings are hedges against inflation, an architect will tell you that a building is its canvas for artistic expression, while the city might say that buildings are functional elements of a community. Well, I would agree with…. all of them, however, my opinion is that a building is a problem, a complicated one. A completed building is a solved problem, it solves a financing problem, a land use problem, a stakeholder satisfaction problem, a fulfillment of demand in a market problem, an aesthetic problem, a design problem, and the list goes on. Next time you look around your community, really observe what is around you and realize that the infrastructure that is enjoyed is the accomplishment of many talented, adventurous, intelligent, and hard-working professionals that dedicate their lives to embellishing communities with services and products. I read somewhere that the world is the museum of humanity's accomplishments, and this especially rings true to real estate.

Through this book I hope to illustrate to you the different disciplines that are involved in the accomplishment of developing a building and what their general responsibilities and thought processes are. You will notice that each professional carries an eye for identifying different issues as well as unique creative methods of solving the problem. With this I hope to provide you some insight into what the real estate work entails and where you might fit in it. The real estate development world thirsts for hard working and gifted professionals like yourself. You will realize that whether you come from a business background, (i.e., marketing, accounting, finance) or a more construction related background (i.e. engineering, architecture, or construction management) or are even just barely looking at the real estate development world as a career path, this book is for you. You will still be able to garner much useful information on the nature of the real estate development business and all the "musts" that a deal must undergo to make a sound decision on the acquisition of a site, a pursuit (this is a term that investment teams use to refer to a deal they wish to close on), and what it takes to have a successful development. My goal is to give you insight into the process of a development and the players involved to ensure a successful development occurs.

Furthermore, I wish to use this book as a warm welcome to the industry by exposing you to key terms, the process through which deals are closed, and the players involved in the process. Before we get into the meat and potatoes of the book, I would like to share with you the way I see real estate development. From my perspective, real estate development is an investment vehicle that encompasses an extravagant array of disciplines which include but are not limited to architecture, engineering, finance, accounting, marketing, construction management, contracting, law, and environmental science to generate wealth for stakeholders as well as the communities in which subject developments are located. Not only does real estate hold the means to generate wealth, but it also possesses the force to shape and form the physical landscapes and living experiences of citizens within a community, city, state, and country! It truly is incredible to think about all the magnificent cities in the world and the substantial role that real estate development plays in their growth.

We will keep the preface short, after all we are all in a hurry! With that, let's jump into it!

Chapter 1:
Know the Players

One of the most important aspects about diving into a new industry is understanding who participates in it and their respective roles. Let's look at a responsibility matrix:

Architecture Team	responsible for leading the design of the project.
Investments Team	responsible for sourcing deals through brokers, financial modeling, as well as sourcing capital (debt & equity).
Pre-Construction Team	responsible for leading due diligence efforts, making sure that the site is shovel ready for construction start, and negotiating out hard costs for construction.
Design Management Team	responsible for managing the architect from an ownership's perspective.
Construction Management Team	responsible for managing the general contractor that will be building the project.
General Contracting Team	responsible for building the project on time and within budget.
Leasing & Marketing Team	responsible for generating market presence and driving leases for the

	building to generate monthly cash flow.
Property Management Team	responsible for managing daily operations of the building.

We will delve into further detail on what each of these teams is responsible for, as you will interact with them on a daily basis and it's important to understand their role within the overarching goal. We will focus on making sure that a concise explanation for each of their duties is outlined. As you will see in your own experience, none of these teams operate in a siloed nature, but rather, they are constantly communicating with each other to make sure that the development's needs are being addressed. Once you enter the real estate world you will see how each element of the project whether it's finance, design, or construction is related to one another. Without further ado, let's begin with the architecture team, the artists of the project.

Chapter 2:
Architecture; The Artists

Architecture Team:

Selecting the correct architect for the project is paramount for the success of a real estate development. As a matter of fact, any consultant or designer that gets brought into the mix plays a substantial role in the success of a deal, so being selective pays off in the future. Some things to consider when evaluating architects would be their relative experience in the city you want to build in, their experience with the specific asset class you are looking to deliver (i.e. multifamily vs. student living vs. industrial vs. senior living vs. office vs. medical office building etc.), as well as their overall fees. The reason to understand the architect's experience in a given location is because different cities have unique design codes, zoning variances, entitlement processes, permitting requirements, and their own idiosyncrasies (as well as similarities). An architect that has a good handle on these things is worth gold as they know the intricacies of the process and can plan for them accordingly into their designs and schedules. Furthermore, having experience in specific localities means that the governmental bodies responsible for approving designs and projects already know the design team which inserts a level of trust that can be leveraged to expediting entitlements and permits, mitigating delays (as well as headaches!).

Understanding the zoning variances, design codes, entitlement, and permitting processes allows the architecture team to fully understand what can be designed and built in the parcel of land that is being looked at by the investments team. This is crucial to understand, since the investments team always needs to take the liberty to make some assumptions in their underwriting at the beginning of the project (underwriting is the process through which the investments team outlines the characteristics of a project they are looking to build such as beds and units and how those affect the monies projected to come into the property once under operation and how it compares to the costs) such as how many floors, beds, units, and square footage is going to be used. Beds and units are the main usual drivers of cash flow in a property so understanding and knowing how many can be built is critical to understanding returns and feasibility for a development. In addition to this, the architect will generate sets of drawings that are in increasing order of detail, as the project keeps progressing towards the construction start date.

Below you can see some exhibits showing the different levels of detail. The illustrations are organized in order of detail from least detailed to most detailed issuance.

1. *Figure 1: Conceptual Set:*

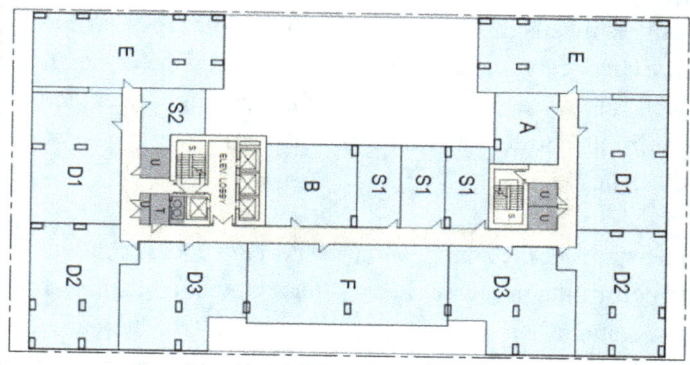

2. *Figure 2: Schematic Set:*

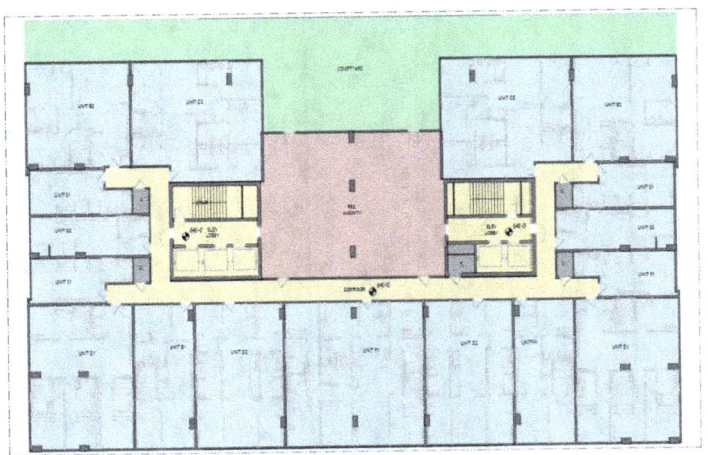

3. *Figure 3: Design Development Set*

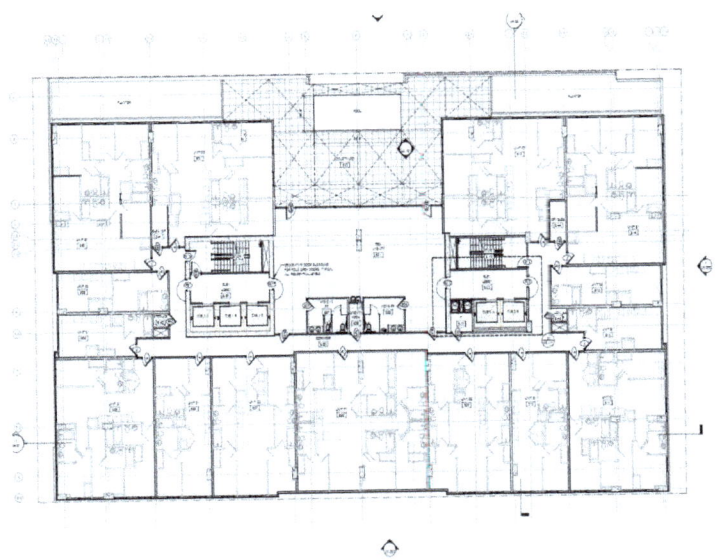

4. *Figure 4: Permit / GMP Set:*

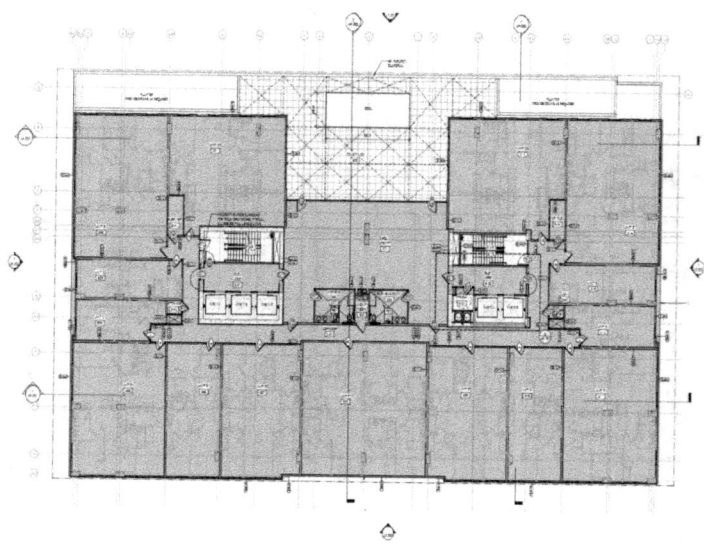

5. *Figure 5: Construction Documents*

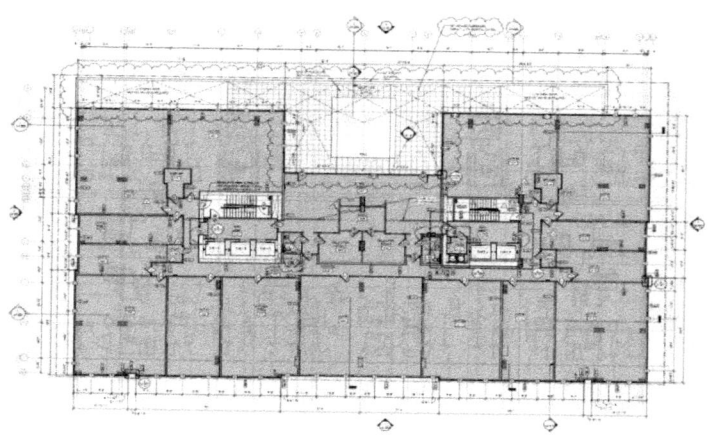

These are the sets that need to be included when analyzing the architect's proposal. In addition to this, the architect is responsible for coordinating the different design disciplines such as mechanical, electrical, plumbing, interiors, landscaping, structural, and civil.

Chapter 3:
Investments; The Dreamers

Investments Team:

In addition to the architecture team, there is the investments team. The investments team is responsible for sourcing deals either through brokers in the respective markets where they are looking to develop or just themselves through their personal connections. They handle all the financial modeling aspects of a project and make sure that the numbers work in the favor of the development. They do this by developing a financial model which is an excel workbook that illustrates all of the costs for the development i.e., pursuit costs, closing costs, soft costs, and hard costs. They model that in comparison to the revenues that the asset is projected to generate. The cash inflow of an asset is dependent on what the market rents are at the time and where the rents are expected to go, rents can go up, down, or stay the same from when the original model was generated. Once they have all the costs and revenues identified, they analyze the deal using various key metrics such as the internal rate of return, known as the IRR, net present value, cash on cash, equity multiple, and any debt metrics. Let's discuss these in a bit of detail just to provide a general understanding of what each metric tells you about the project.

Investments Team & Internal Rate of Return (IRR):

The IRR lets you know what the annual rate of return will be on the building you are looking to develop given the different cash flows expected. It's a great tool to capture the time value of money but it lacks the ability to convey what the overall profits will be or how the returns are distributed between all partners in the deal. In order to calculate the IRR in excel, you would use either the "=IRR()" function or the "=XIRR()" function. If you have an idea of the dates in which you expect to incur cash outflows and the dates you expect to receive cash inflows then I recommend the "=XIRR()" function be used.

Investments Team & Net Present Value (NPV):

The NPV is a useful tool to determine what the costs and revenues of a development are worth today. A dollar today is not the same as a dollar tomorrow, a week, a month, or a year from now due to the uncertainty of the future. The way that we get rewarded for holding onto a dollar in an investment vehicle, for taking on the uncertainty of the future, is by earning interest on it. This same logic applies to when analysts are taking a look at revenues and costs of a building. The investments team will analyze all the costs expected to be incurred in the future as well as all the revenues to be received in the future and come up with what they are worth today. In theory, if the net present value is greater than 0, then the investment is worth pursuing, if it's 0 then we would be indifferent about the investment, and if it's less than 0 we would walk away from the investment. The NPV can be easily calculated in excel as well, using the "=NPV()" function, however, the math behind the NPV function wasn't correctly coded and it will actually give you the present value of the cash flows. In order to account for this, we would just subtract the costs incurred on day 0 to get the NPV.

Investments Team & Equity Multiple (EM):

As we mentioned before the IRR fails to measure the overall profitability of an investment. The equity multiple is able to capture that as well as how many times an investment pays back the equity that was invested. One of the shortcomings of the metric is that it doesn't capture time value of money (the notion that a dollar today is not worth the same as a dollar tomorrow). To calculate the equity multiple, we do the following: (total profit + peak equity)/peak equity.

Investments Team & Cash-on-cash (CoC):

Cash on cash provides insight into the annual cash return on an investment and summarizes the cash distributions through the term of the investment. If you remember the IRR fails to show the actual cash on the return it just shows it on a % basis. This metric can easily be calculated by doing the following: annual cash income/peak equity.

Investments Team & Debt Metrics:

Some, albeit not all, of the debt metrics that the investment team use are the debt service coverage and the debt yield. Debt service coverage is important to understand as this will inform the group on whether or not the property generates enough cash flows to cover the loan payments that need to be made. This is easily calculated with the following formula: Net Operating Income (NOI)/(Interest + Amortization). Debt yield is just the cash flow relative to the total loan amount, this is calculated with the following formula: Annualized NOI / Loan Balance. It is imperative that all the costs that the investments team have modeled be updated continually. The reason being is that the costs and revenues are usually assumptions, generally speaking very good assumptions, but all assumptions are always imperfect. Updating the models and informing the investment teams of where the actual costs are coming in on a pursuit is important to keep an eye on how the metrics outlined above change. Generally speaking, some of the costs make up a very low percentage of the overall capital required so being off on an assumption is not a deal killer. The most important cost item in the proforma is the hard cost. This cost is the cost to build the project and accounts for most of the capital that will be used in the development so having an informed hard cost number in the financial model is key for success.

Investments Team & The Capital Stack:

You might have noticed two terms from the metrics that were previously mentioned: equity and debt. The investments team is responsible for sourcing funds to build the development and funds can come from two different avenues; equity, and debt. Equity can be simply thought of as "ownership" of the project. This ownership is reflected using dollar signs of course and this would represent a certain percentage of the total amount of money used to build the development. Equity can come from within the developer's own pockets, but it can also come from third parties, equity partners. Equity partners are usually investment funds that are looking to invest in different ventures. It is typical for the investments team within the development firm to model their finances assuming equity to be broken out in between the equity partner and their own (the developer's) financial resources. For an equity partner to be onboard with investing in the project, they would need to study the returns and see if the benefit is worth taking on the risk. However, once they provide funds, they become partners in the project and they own and are entitled to a certain percentage of the returns generated by the project. Debt on the other hand is different in nature. Debt comes from lenders. Lenders don't take ownership of the project but expect the recipient of the loan to pay the loan back in full plus a bit extra for taking the risk of lending out their money. Another term for debt is "leverage," which is used to refer to the usage of debt within the project. Real Estate is one of the most "leveraged" assets in the world; typically deals will be composed of twenty percent equity and eighty percent debt. One might wonder why organizations, like banks, would be willing to provide that much funding for a project. One of the reasons is that real estate is a very tangible asset so it's easy for banks to understand where the money is going to be placed. Additionally, if the loan is not paid back, the bank could just take the building so "collateral" is easily understood and outlined in any loan agreements. From the developer's perspective, one might think: "Why would I ever take that much debt?" There are multiple reasons but the one that I think is the most practical is that it frees one's own funds to make more deals. Think about it this way; let's say building a house costs one hundred dollars and you have exactly that amount of money. This means you can only build one house with pure "equity." Is there a way to build ten houses with one hundred dollars? This would be possible using debt instruments, so you could get a loan for ninety dollars on each of the ten houses and you would only pay ten dollars to build each house. Using debt allows you to use your equity much more efficiently and build ten houses instead of one with the same one hundred dollars in your pocket. There are multiple sources for debt but the most typical loan types come from the list below and they all have different characteristics:

- Bank loans
    - Debt tolerance: average
    - Leverage: average
    - Rate: average
- Agency loans
    - Debt tolerance: low
    - Leverage: average
    - Rate: low
- Lifeco loans
    - Debt tolerance: very low
    - Leverage: low
    - Rate: low
- CMBS loans
    - Debt tolerance: low
    - Leverage: average
    - Rate: low
- Debt fund loans
    - Debt tolerance: high
    - Leverage: high
    - Rate: high

As you can see these different types of lending avenues have different characteristics as to how much they are willing to lend and at which rates. The lower the rate the better for the developer but from the lender's perspective the more they lend the riskier the project is so they would expect a higher rate, hence a higher return. The next question would be how much the project can afford to be leveraged, in other words, what amount of money we should borrow. This determination is known as loan sizing. Loan sizing is used to determine the maximum supportable loan amount based on the property's net operating income. Net operating income is the income generated by the property on a monthly basis and the question boils down to will the monthly income generated by the property be enough to cover the loan payment.

When it comes to loans there are three key metrics that need to be readily understood. Loan to value, debt service coverage ratio, and debt yield. These can be understood per the below:

- Loan to Value = loan amount / value
    o A lower loan to value would reflect less risk
    o The key here is to understand how the lender defines "value"
- Debt Service Cover Ratio = cash flow / debt service
    o This measures how much cashflow the property has to make loan payments
    o A higher debt service cash ratio equals less risk
    o Understanding what is included in the debt service cover ratio calculation by the lender is important
- Debt Yield = cash flow / loan amount
    o Measures an asset's cash flow relative to the total amount of the loan
    o A higher debt yield reflects less risk

Understanding all of the above in tandem will assist in the determination of how much debt can be afforded to be used. There are other funding mechanisms aside from the more traditional options. Some of these are holdbacks, earnouts, and future fundings. A holdback is a way of funding in which the entire loan is funded upfront except for a small portion of it which is held in escrow (an escrow account is an account within a bank in which funds are held and released only when specific criteria specified, or outcome has been met). An earnout, is a lending mechanism in which not all the money gets funded at the same time, the loan can get increased, but it would be contingent on an agreed event happening. Additionally, there is future funding, this is additional funding that is agreed between the lender and recipient of the loan for specific uses such as new leases, leasing commissions, and tenant improvements.

Regardless of whatever method is used to secure a loan for a project, one must understand a couple of financial terms. The very first item to discuss would be the loan documents. Loan documents are part of every loan, and they outline multiple items such as the different ratios that will be used (some of these we have already discussed) like loan to purchase price, loan to cost, and loan to value. Whichever one is used will largely depend on the nature of the project i.e., building acquisition vs. building development. Interest rates will be discussed within the loan documents. There are really two common interest rates: fixed rates and floating rates. Fixed rates are fixed throughout the period of the loan; this method typically ends in higher rates. Floating rates are interest rates that have the ability to change throughout the duration of the loan. This strategy typically ends with lower interest rates.

There are pros and cons to both rate strategies. Fixed rates, even though they tend to be higher, provide the luxury of eliminating interest rate uncertainty from the equation. Regardless of whether the economy is going through an expansionary or contractionary period, the interest rate of the loan won't change. However, there are times in which interest rates diminish due to the economic forces of the time and in this instance having a floating rate would provide the benefit of allowing the interest rate to be diminished.

Let's talk about how the interest payment would be calculated. Within the loan documents there will be a portion dedicated to outlining how the interest rate payments would be determined. There are multiple ways of calculating these payments. The following three are fairly common:

- 30/60
- Actual over 365
- Actual over 360

The "30/60" method assumes that there are 360 days in the year and ends with the least amount of interest paid. In order to calculate the daily rate one would just divide the annual rate by three hundred and sixty and in order to calculate the monthly rate one can just multiply the daily rate by thirty. The "actual over 365" method assumes that there are 365 days in a year and considers the actual number of days in each month. Similarly, to the "30/60" method, in order to calculate the daily rate, one takes the annual rate and divides by three hundred and sixty five and the monthly rate is found by multiplying the daily rate by thirty. The "actual over 360" method assumes that there are three hundred and sixty days in a year and considers the actual number of days. This results in the highest amount of interest paid and it's the most common method of calculating interest payments. Additionally, the loan documents will outline other items like the term of the loan, fees, recourse, and prepayment penalties. The term of the loan is simply the amount of time that the loan can remain outstanding. This really depends on many things but some of the items that can influence the term of the loan are the type of lender, business plan, and loan type.

The fees outlined will be part of the deal with the borrower. Some of the fees outlined would be any loan origination fee (typically 1% of the loan amount), extension fees (typically in between 0-1% of the loan amount), pay off fee (typically 0-1% of the loan amount), and any other miscellaneous i.e., underwriting, loan application, and third party fees. Additionally, and one that needs special attention, is the outlining of the recourse policy within the loan. There can be a non-recourse clause or a recourse clause. Non-recourse simply means that the loan is collateralized by the property only and not personal assets. Recourse clauses allow for the bank to collateralize a loan against the property and the borrower's personal assets. Finally, prepayment penalties. There are times where it might be worth it to pay off the loan prior to the loan maturation. One might think, "Why would there be a penalty for paying off the loan early?" The reason that lenders charge for prepayment penalties is because they have loaned the borrowers a specific amount at a specific rate for a predetermined amount of time. If the loan gets paid back early, the lender will have to accommodate the same amount of money in another investment which will take money and time as well as risk the money again and not receive the same return. In other words, prepayment penalties compensate the lender to replace the collateral and allow the lender to have the same return.

Once the loan and equity amounts have been established, then a capital stack has been formed. I think it's worth mentioning that there are different categories of debt within debt and equity that are used. The following are the typical categories of debt and equity:

- Senior debt - standard mortgage, largest piece of the pie, usually secured by the property, least risky position, lowest interest rate
- Mezzanine debt - bridges gap between senior debt and equity, gets paid after senior lender, higher interest rate but lower return than equity. Typically has the right to foreclose on the equity position and take control of the property
- Preferred equity - senior only to common equity, gets paid after senior and mezz lenders, returns vary and include upside participation
- Common equity - often smallest piece of capital, ownership of the property, most risky position, and greatest potential return

As you can see the way that the financing capital stack can be put together varies quite a bit but at the end of the day it's composed of equity and debt. Now let's discuss a bit about how each piece of capital gets compensated for being invested in the project.

Chapter 4:
Joint Ventures & Waterfalls; Dealmakers

Joint Ventures:

Joint Ventures or "JVs" are agreements between two entities in which both entities decide to pull resources together to acquire a piece of land and develop it. If you think about it, purchasing land and developing it requires a substantial number of resources. With that in consideration, it makes sense that joint ventures be enacted as the main vehicle of developing real estate deals as it spreads the risk in between the two entities with the benefit of added resources. As a result, most real estate developments are joint ventures. Within the joint ventures there are typically two entities, the limited partner (LP) and general partner (GP). The way to think about these two entities is the following: the limited partner is an investor and is not involved in the day-to-day operations of the business, in this case real estate development. However, they bring cash into the deal. The general partner can be thought of as the operator of the business; the general partner brings in a comparatively small amount of cash to the table as well as experience and "know how" to the deal in order to make the project a reality. The capital breakdown between two entities typically falls within the 90/10 or 80/20 split (LP/GP). This relationship is governed by legal documents typically known as JV Agreements and they will outline the rights and responsibilities of each entity. Some items outlined on these agreements are the following.

- Control & Decision Rights
- Shares of Invested Equity / Equity Splits
- Distribution of Profits
- Management and Responsibilities

As you can see, understanding the nature of the JV agreement is crucial for a successful development but also for fostering relationships that could possibly lead to future deals with the limited partner.

Waterfalls & Profit Distribution:

A waterfall is a method of unevenly allocating profits in between the partners in the deal. When it comes to profit distribution it is important to understand that there is a hierarchy of repayment. First of all, debt needs to be repaid so lenders are the first ones to be compensated hence they are the ones that carry less risk and consequently earn a lower pre-determined return. Subsequently, equity gets repaid, since their position is second to the lender, they take more risk so their return fluctuates on how well the development performs. Finally, the general partner or operator is paid whatever is left. Therefore, metaphorically speaking, the arrangement is called a waterfall. As the "water" (cash) fills up and overflows the debt pool, any excess falls to the equity pool, and any excess from the equity pool spills over to the general partner's pool. This waterfall structure is not only a method to distribute profits, but it is also a tool for risk management. This is true because the downside risk is carried away from the lenders and the equity partners (since they get paid first) and the general partner burdens the risk of being compensated last. However, the upside potential is given to the general partner/operator for taking the risk of being the last one paid with the chance to earn disproportionately more from the limited amount invested. This allows for an alignment of interest in which the lenders and equity partners incentivize the general partner to manage and deliver the project in the most profitable manner. If the general partner delivers, the lender gets paid, the equity partner gets paid, and the general partner makes some real money.

The incentive for the general partner to make this disproportionate return on the investment is called the "promote." In order for the general partner/operator to make this "promote," it must first clear what is termed the hurdle rate. The hurdle rate is the return in which the cash flow distribution changes in between the equity partner and the general partner/operator. This can be illustrated and digested with an example. This can easily be explained with an example, let's say that an investor invests ninety percent of a $1 million dollar project ($900,000) and the other ten percent is equity from the developer ($100,000). There is a preferred rate of eight percent (this is usually the IRR that's agreed upon in the agreement with the investor) which means that on any return up to eight percent the split in profits is ninety percent for the investor and ten percent for the developer. This means that if the project gets a return of eight percent the first year ($80,000) then ninety percent would go to the investor ($72,000) and ten percent ($8,000) would go to the developer. Now let us say that it is agreed that after any excess in return after the eight percent up to fifteen percent the developer will get thirty percent of the return and the investor will get seventy percent of the return. So, let's say that the second year the return is fifteen percent ($150,000). This means that on the first eight percent the profits ($80,000) will be split like before (ten percent to the developer and ninety percent to the investor). Since the returns pass the first hurdle rate of eight percent, the developer is entitled to a "promote" and as we said previously the "promote" will be thirty percent to the developer and seventy percent to the investor. In this case there are seventy thousand dollars left ($70,000) to be split and per the "promote" the developer will end up getting thirty percent of that ($21,000) and the investor will get seventy percent ($49,000). Typically, there are multiple "promotes" and with each increasing hurdle rate the more money the developer can make.

As you can see this is where the developer has a great opportunity to make a substantial amount of money without having to risk much of its own capital. This is what is called making money using other people's money. Furthermore, you can see why this is a great risk mitigation tactic and incentive structure that the investor looks to have in place with developers; waterfalls incentivize developers to work arduously in order to ensure that the development achieves not only the preferred return but also a larger return which would simultaneously allow for the investor to earn the required return while allowing for the developer to make the most money possible.

As you can see the way that these structures are modeled alongside the terms of the joint venture agreement will really be a driving factor on whether the deal becomes a reality or not, therefore "promotes," hurdle rates, returns, and joint ventures are deal makers for any developers.

Chapter 5:
Pre-Construction;
The Detectives

Pre-Construction Team:

The pre-construction team is tasked with multiple responsibilities, those of which include managing and leading of due diligence efforts in the early stages of a project as well as coordinating any construction activities to prep a site for construction start, essentially leaving a site "shovel ready" for the general contractor to have a smooth mobilization. The pre-construction team plays an integral role in assisting the investments team in understanding the risk profile of a project from a technical perspective. Here are some of the aspects that are analyzed by the pre-construction team albeit not all are listed: environmental conditions on site (i.e. contaminated soils), geotechnical conditions (i.e. structural quality of soils), easements and property lines on site, as well as any utilities around the property. The extent of due diligence work that will need to be conducted on a site is contingent on the complexity of the site. Let's jump into the typical due diligence items that should always be completed by a pre-construction team.

Environmental Site Assessments (ESA):

Environmental site assessments play a key role in understanding if there will be any remediation costs associated with the site in play or if there will be a need to engineer and implement contamination mitigation systems into the building. For starters, the pre-construction team reaches out to various environmental engineers searching for the best price in the market to conduct environmental site assessments. The first assessment of the site is called a Phase I ESA. Phase I ESAs are passive assessments of the property in question, meaning there is no actual sampling of the present materials on-site. From this report, the pre-construction team will garner information regarding past uses of the property, ownership history, incident history, and many other pieces of information. What the team is truly looking to uncover is if there are any RECs on-site. REC stands for "recognized environmental conditions". A good example of a recognized environmental condition would be that the site in question was previously used as a gas station and there is record of underground storage tanks being used on the site to store gasoline.

This is considered a REC since the possibility of the underground storage tank leaking and contaminating the soils exists. For the most part, if a REC is found onsite, further investigation will be warranted. An example of a list of RECs can be found below:

Figure 6: Recognized Environmental Conditions

- **REC** - The site's historical usage (auto service center) in the 1940s and 1950s, use of petroleum products and automotive repair-related chemicals, potential for subsurface equipment (hydraulic lifts) is considered a REC due to the potential for an undocumented, historical release of hazardous substances and/or petroleum products.

- **REC** - The presence of over 100 LUST and SLIC listings reported within one-half mile of the site indicates a higher likelihood of off-site releases of hazardous materials and/or petroleum products potentially impacting groundwater at the site. Several adjacent properties had unauthorized releases that impacted groundwater in the site vicinity, and potentially the site. Low concentrations of chlorinated VOCs were detected at several nearby properties and the source(s) of the VOCs is unknown.

- **REC** - Due to the historical development of the site since the late 1800s and long-term industrial and commercial usage in the downtown area, there is a potential for undocumented USTs (e.g., heating purposes) to be present, cisterns, septic systems, and burned wastes, lead, or other metals to be present in shallow soil, especially debris-containing fill soil.

If a REC is encountered, a phase II ESA will be required to be conducted. A Phase II ESA is an active assessment of the conditions onsite. This is when the environmental engineer will go out to site and take soils, groundwater, and soil gas samples to run them through different analysis and determine if these are in fact contaminated. If contamination is encountered, a strategy will need to be devised by the pre-construction manager and the environmental engineers to manage the issue. The strategy to be instituted is contingent on multiple requirements from the various regulatory entities involved some of which include, albeit not all, the requirements of capital partners, city, state, department of environmental quality and your firm's internal required procedures and best practices. The pre-construction management team's responsibility is to ensure that all requirements are incorporated into the development's environmental strategy in order to assure that proper time is allocated for any regulatory processes and that costs to go through these processes are accounted for.

This responsibility not only falls solely on the shoulders of the development firm's pre-construction team but the environmental engineer as well. If contaminated soils were found onsite, then a soils management plan will need to be in place before construction starts. A soils management plan is just as it sounds, a plan devised by the environmental engineer to manage the handling and disposal of contaminated soils offsite. Developers need to have a keen understanding on the nature of this plan as it can be costly depending on the nature of the building to be built, type of contamination encountered, and the sheer size of the impacted area onsite. One item to keep an eye out for is the need for a project to receive an NFA letter. An NFA stands for "No Further Action" letter, which is a letter issued by the local jurisdiction stating that the developer has taken care of the contamination onsite and that there is, you guessed it, no further action necessary to remediate the site.

One other element to keep an eye out for is the presence of an existing structure on your site. Typically, the sites that the investments team is looking to purchase are pieces of land that have been developed in the past with either a commercial building or a single-family home or a mixture of both. Information about the existing structures onsite will be outlined in the phase I ESA and it's imperative to understand the nature of the materials used in the building. The reason being is that if there is an existing building onsite you will more than likely need to demolish it. In order to demolish it, you as the developer, will need to assure the city that no existing contaminant particles that could be in the building will sparse out into the wider community through the demolition efforts and cause a health concern. In fact, the city won't issue your contractor the permit to demolish the building if there is no record of the removal of hazardous materials from the building.

In order to ensure that all hazardous materials are removed, you as the developer, need to conduct a hazardous materials survey of the building. This survey will identify if any hazardous materials were used in the construction of the building, typically lead based paint and asbestos are the main culprits in this survey. This survey is typically completed by the environmental engineer that completed the phase I ESA. Consequently, this survey will be shared with either an abatement (abatement is the process of removing the hazardous materials from the building) or demolition contractor. It is worth noting that there are times in which the demolition contractor has the capacity to complete abatement work. If that is the case, then I would recommend to complete the abatement under his contract as this will eliminate the need of bringing someone else into the project and will simultaneously ensure that the work is completed by a contractor that will be familiar with the project.

American Land Title Association (ALTA) Survey:

These surveys are instrumental to understanding what the existing conditions of the site are. It provides information about where the property lines are located, set back requirements, easements, utilities as well as many other elements. All of the aforementioned items are critical in determining if the assumed size of the project will "fit" in the prospective site. This is critical to understand, as the size of the building dictates how many units and beds can be built into the project; the more beds and units, the more cash flow generated by the property. Not all ALTA surveys are the same as there are multiple options or elements that can be chosen to be included in the survey depending on what type of information you as the developer are trying to understand. These options come from the "Table A," which is a table that itemizes all the pieces of information that could be incorporated into the survey. This table can be found online and it is public information. Note that all of the "Table A" items are not necessarily needed at the very beginning of the project. This means that the right tension in between money and the amount of information required to understand the risk profile of the site needs to be determined. Some elements that can typically be found as options in the "Table A" would be property lines, sets of permanent monuments, easements, topography, elevations, onsite utilities, offsite utilities, and many other items. When kicking off due diligence for a site, the topography might not be of much need, especially if you have seen the site and it's relatively flat, which means that if you have a limited amount of money to spend you might want to defer the collection of site topography until the deal is in more solid ground. Afterall you don't want to spend substantial amounts of money on a deal that has a low probability of moving forward. An example of a survey with multiple easements can be observed below:

Figure 7: ALTA Easement Identification

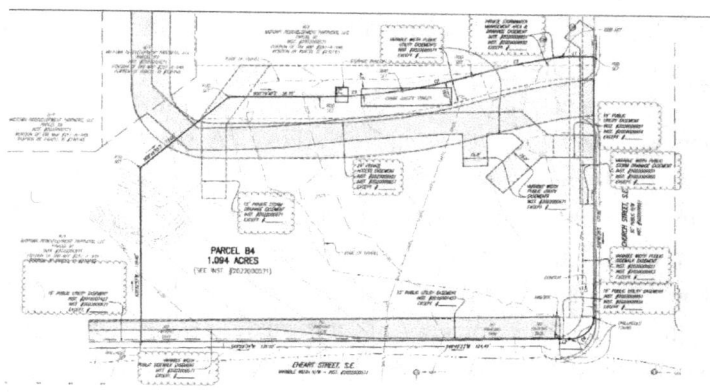

One thing to keep in the back of your mind when looking at surveys, especially when having projects that are characterized by "zero-lot line conditions" (meaning the buildings are property line to property line next to each other, e.g., think of New York or Chicago where buildings are physically touching each other), is understanding how the existing buildings abutting your project impact the development. There are times when the adjacent buildings are encroaching into the open piece of land where you are looking to develop. This needs to be taken into consideration to understand how much square feet is available in the piece of land, where the foundations of the existing building are located, and obviously how this will be managed during the distinct design phases.

Geotechnical Investigation:

This type of investigation is one of the key investigations for a site as the information encountered will be used across the design cycle of the structural drawings for the development. These reports will reveal to the project information about the project and what design and construction measures will need to be taken into consideration when designing and constructing the building. The measures that would be recommended in the geotechnical report are in a way contingent on the type of building the investments team is thinking of raising capital for. The soils encountered will have certain characteristics but the design recommendations will come in relation to the type of structure and how it would interact with the soils on site. That is to say, there are excellent soils and there are awful soils but for the most part, different engineering techniques can be employed to design and build a building on excellent soils or not so excellent soils. As it was aforementioned, the type of building to be built matters in relation to the geotechnical investigation. For example, height of the building, use of the building, parking at grade level, underground parking, basements, parking garage, and overall footprint for the building are items that will guide the Geotech investigation.

For example, the overall footprint of the building will inform us where we should be drilling to get soil information (we wouldn't want to drill in an area where the building won't be supported), basement, underground parking considerations, and height of the building provides us with direction on how deep we have to drill into the soil. The reason being is that if we have a 40-story high rise, we are likely going to need deep foundations (caissons & piles) compared to if we have a 5 story mid-rise in which we would only need shallow foundations (footings & mat slabs). It is important to note that the deeper we drill to acquire soil data the more expensive the investigation becomes. Once drilling is completed, the geotechnical engineer will provide a report in which he will summarize the findings and provide design recommendations to the structural engineer. Recommendations will be for structural elements such as footing dimensions, safety factors, pile dimensions, depth of foundations, friction coefficients, shear wave analysis, site classification as well as construction techniques such as dewatering procedures, soil compaction rates, soil underlayment preparation, and rock excavation.

Furthermore, a thing to keep an eye out for is the location where the project is located. It's always important to keep in mind that there are earthquake zones and along with earthquakes come faults. Fault zones and earthquakes are very common in the west coast of the United States, and they need to be taken seriously throughout the life cycle of the project in order to understand their impact on your development. This effort to understand seismic activity on your site is part of the geotechnical investigation. Faults might be an item that could kill the development if one is encountered on your site as different municipalities have stringent requirements that must be adhered to if building in a zone riddled with faults. For example, in San Diego, in order to build a project in a fault zone, the developer must prove to the city that all existing active faults are twenty-five feet away from the building. If this is not the case, the City of San Diego will not approve the development and construction of the project.

Additionally, there are other scenarios that might impact your project's budget and design efforts such as shallow bedrock, which can be very expensive to remove if a basement is required. Liquefaction probability is another major risk, which is when soils behave like liquids for a split second due to high moisture content in the soil, which if you can imagine is not great if you have a building on top. A nice analogy to liquified soils would be if you tried to build a house on a pool filled with water, you probably wouldn't want to live in that house! Although you would have a pool, so the choice is yours. An example of a boring log can be found on figure 8.

Figure 8: Example of Geotechnical Boring Log

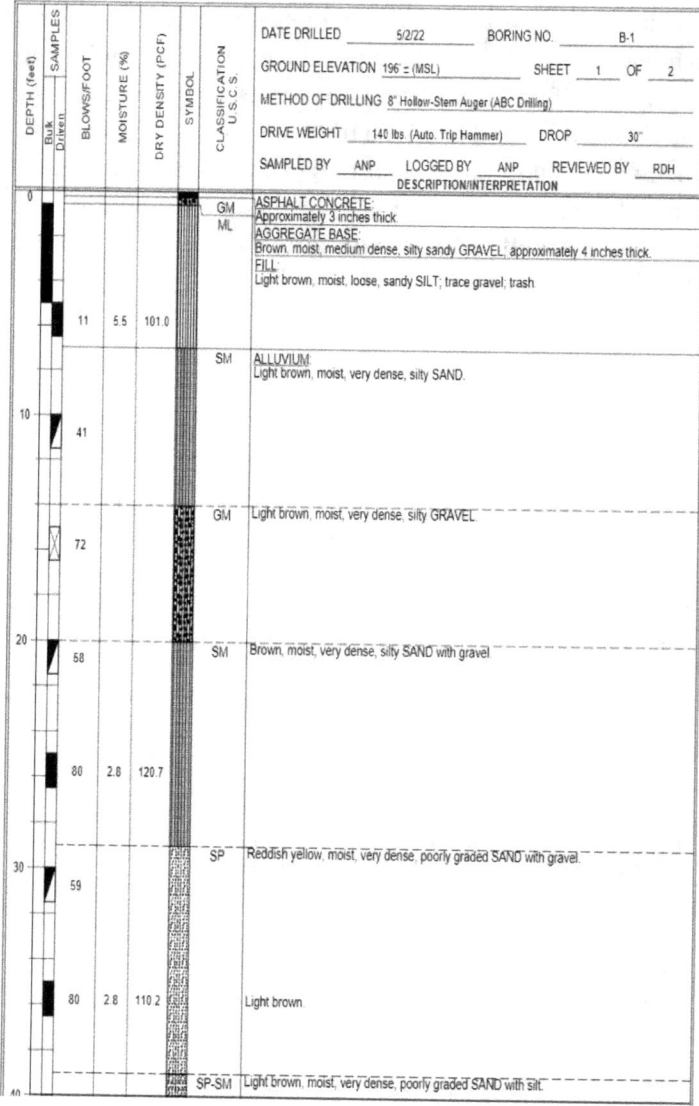

Property Condition Assessments:

As we have mentioned before, existing properties on site can be problematic for the development. We have discussed the investigations that would need to be conducted from an environmental perspective if the intent is to demolish the existing building/structure. If we wish to keep the existing building/structure onsite and re-model and re-program for a different usage, then we would still need to do a hazardous materials survey because construction activities will be happening. Additionally, we would need to understand the condition of the building and if its current stance carries with the appropriate infrastructure to serve its new use. This is when a property condition assessment will need to be completed. This report will provide insight into the stance of the following:

1. Conditions of Mechanical Systems
2. Conditions of Electrical Systems
3. Conditions of Plumbing Systems
4. Conditions of Structural Systems
5. Conditions of Hazardous Materials
6. Conditions of Roof
7. Conditions of Floor Finishes
8. Conditions of Wall Finishes
9. Conditions of Appliances

There are many other items that would be encompassed in this type of report and it's important to understand what is in fairly good shape and what other items have decayed so much that would need to be replaced or repaired. These repairs can rapidly increase in cost expensive and if they are not anticipated into the overall project budget from the get-go, then there will be serious deficiencies in the finances of the project. The property assessment report should come with an overview of what the issues found onsite and what the estimated budget is to either replace or repair the identified deficiency. If this is something that the consultant is not willing to provide, then I would strongly recommend pivoting into finding another consultant, assuming there is time to do so. Let's move into understanding how utilities can potentially impact the project.

Will Serve Letters:

First and foremost, the developer needs to get an understanding of what utility services are in the area. In highly dense areas like major metropolitan cities, it might be fairly simple to assure that there will be utility services and infrastructure available for your project to be served by; however, this is not the case if the project is located in a more remote area of the country. One note of caution for developments in major metropolitan areas: while it is true that major infrastructure will be available, it is important to understand if the utility infrastructure present has the capacity to take in the additional demand generated by your development. In some instances, depending on the scale of the project, a major infrastructure improvement effort will need to take place to serve the building. These major infrastructure improvements can be costly and time consuming, so they are important to identify early on and make sure that the development team is aware of them. The developer needs to reach out to the local utility companies in the area and do some due diligence to understand if the electrical, gas, water, sewer, and telecommunications demand of the project can be handled by the existing infrastructure capacity. For every development you undertake, you will want to have a will serve letter for the following:

1. Electrical
2. Gas
3. Telecommunications
4. Water
5. Sewer

Utility Relocation:

When it comes to utilities, it is very likely that there will be some utilities crossing the site you are looking to develop, especially if there is an existing building on it such as a single-family home. As the developer, it will be your responsibility to ensure that the lines in the way of construction are relocated or removed. Typically, this is the case with overhead power lines and telecommunication lines. The process to remove these lines or relocate them is not a complicated one but it is a time intensive endeavor. Utility companies are notorious for delaying construction companies due to their lack of responses, understaffing, and lack of communication skills. The approach to relocating versus removing overhead lines is contingent on the nature of the project and how these overhead lines affect the project. The first step would be to assess the property and understand what will need to be done to relocate or remove the lines and apprehend an idea on the timing of these activities. Consequently, you as the developer will need to contact the local power company and the telecom provider that are on the pole and start a conversation about your project. This will kick off the internal conversations within the respective groups and your project will be in the know. Once this occurs, the project will go under review and be scheduled for engineering, at which point you will likely be asked to cover a design fee. Once engineering is complete, the project will be scheduled for construction and removal. The typical timeline for this process to go to fruition is anywhere in between 6-8 months, which is why identifying the need for relocation early in the project is crucial to a healthy construction schedule. It is worth noting that the power company might not own the poles in which the lines are running through so uncovering who has ownership of the poles is imperative to assure that there are no scope gaps. Most of the utility relocation work developers encounter is with power and telecom lines but gas lines can be in the way as well.

Permanent Service Design:

Developers are always responsible for coordinating power and gas service to the development. The civil engineer doesn't typically develop the engineering for dry utilities such as gas and electrical service, but the engineer will coordinate its design with the engineering plans of the respective utility companies; however, civil engineers do take ownership of developing the wet utilities for the project. Akin to the utility relocation effort, the permanent design effort is not an overly complicated one but it can take an exorbitant amount of time. Once the project has well defined gas loads and electrical loads, you as the developer, will have to share those with the utility companies. They might ask for additional questions such as a site plan or single line diagrams. It is important to respond with any requests by the utility company in a timely fashion. An element of coordination that befalls the owner is the location of the permanent service equipment that will be needed for the project. This is in regard to the location of transformers, generators, meters, etc. Placing transformers on a site can be problematic if there is not much space. My personal recommendation is to always look to place the transformers in a place outside of the building open to the sky. The reason being is that power companies typically have access requirements to transformers as well as multiple minimum clearances that need to be met in order for them to approve a location. Placing the transformer outside of the building in an area open to the sky simplifies things as it will meet most of the requirements. If there is no space within the confines of the property then it will need to go inside the building or underneath the sidewalk. Different power companies have different requirements to be met in these conditions so make sure the designer is taking them into consideration. One thing to keep in mind is that the power company will not be placing their equipment if they do not have an easement (an easement is simply a right given by a property owner to a third party to be in their property, this is a typical legal instrument that utility companies employ to reduce their risk) for it on your property. This means that an easement will need to be drawn up by a surveyor, at your expense, and recorded by the power company prior to installation of their equipment on site. As mentioned previously this process can take a long time as well. This can range from 6-8 months to coordinate and might go well into construction. Construction schedules typically don't require permanent power until the elevators are going to be installed, however, having permanent power onsite sooner rather than later is best. This brings up an important question: if permanent power doesn't play a role until months into the construction schedule, then how does the general contractor have electricity for lighting and powering his tools and equipment? Temp power.

Temp Power:

Temporary power is one of the items that needs to be coordinated in order to assure that the general contractor has a source of power for his tools and equipment. A major piece of equipment that will require access to power is the tower crane. If a tower crane will be used on site then having temporary power for it in advance of installation is paramount. This process is similar to the permanent and relocation service design efforts. Its timeline is somewhat less but it's still in the months range, taking 4-6 months to complete.

Chapter 6:
Design Management;
The Boundaries

Design Management Team:

Some development groups are experienced enough to recognize the value of integrating a design management team. Design Management teams work as the boundaries or "horse blinders" for the architects and engineers of the project if you will. The design management team is in place to assure that the goals for the building that the investments team needs are made a reality. This team works in tandem with the pre-construction team to assure that the correct design information is divulged to the different design parties in the project. As mentioned previously in chapter 3, this team works with the investments team to coordinate the spatial requirements that would suit required unit mix to generate enough cash flow for the project. Additionally, they work closely with the designers guiding their "pencils" along the right path to assure that the product being designed is of the expected quality and within the appropriate construction cost range. Understanding that the design phase is one of the most important stages of the project is critical, this is the time to drive changes and explore different design ideas to find the fastest and most cost-effective solution.

Design disciplines are always open to criticism from other players in the process. There are the comments from the design management team in order to direct the design in the desired direction, but there is also the opinion of the city in which the project will be developed. If you have spent any time in the development, you will see that making sure that the comments and concerns of city officials are integrated into the project is key to making sure the project is approved for construction. Hence, it follows that comments provided by the different city officials are foundational to having a smooth process with the city as well as crucial to fostering relationships in cities where future developments are likely to occur. From my perspective, this is one of the most challenging hurdles the design management team encounters in their careers. They are the ones in charge of making sure the ownership group is comfortable with the product, that the pre-construction team is comfortable with the constructability and affordability of the product, and that all the different city department heads are inspired by the development being proposed.

Design Managers & Cities:

Let's discuss the third element, inspiring city departments. It is important to understand that city officials in charge of overseeing their city's development have one very important job, to protect and drive the vision for the growth of their city. They work arduously to assure that their city's grow in an organized manner, assuring public goods such as roads, parks, sidewalks, and schools are affected in a generally positive manner with each approved development. Additionally, they safeguard the architectural character of their cities. Incorporating the general architectural character of the city into one's development as well as showing to the city that you have taken them and their constituents into account is a way to get city officials excited for the development. Furthermore, the different offices within the organism of the city are also looking for economic development, essentially, they want to understand how the project would economically impact their communities. Will this development generate jobs? If so, will it be only during construction, or will the building be operated? Will the development bring in any big name players like Amazon or Tesla into the mix (sometimes this is desirable by the city, sometimes it isn't, do your research)? Will the development generate any property tax revenue or permit/impact fee revenue to support public services such as public schools, fire departments, police departments, parks & recreation (think of Leslie Knope & Ron Swanson), and whatever other public goods might come into play? In essence, good city officials are and should be wardens of order and beauty in their cities.

Design Managers & Pre-Construction:

As you can see, there are multiple factors that need to be taken into consideration when the design is being put together and the design managers are burdened to incorporate everything just mentioned and more into a design that's realistic, affordable, and elegant. Let's discuss the design manager's interaction with the pre-construction team and how they work together to arrive at an affordable project. We previously discussed the architecture's team role in designing the different levels of detailed drawings (conceptual, schematic, design development, permit/GMP set, construction documents). Well, as the project moves through the different design stages, the pre-construction team is constantly pricing the project with general contractors in the localities in which the development will be situated. As the drawings get priced up in the "streets," the pre-construction team garners information on what is expensive and what is not so expensive (everything is expensive you just have to find what is the least expensive - it's not easy). Some examples of the changes that occur are the following (this is by no means an exhaustive list as there are many more potential changes in play):

1. Facade materials
2. Weatherproofing
3. Window sizes & types
4. Finishes
5. Light fixtures

As this information is garnered it is also simultaneously communicated to the design managers for them to coordinate material changes in the project with the architect. As the drawings progress through their different stages, pricing keeps being updated, which means that as time goes on, the pricing starts to become more and more realistic. It's imperative that as pricing changes that the investments team is made aware. At the end of the day, the investments team is in charge of making sure that there is enough money in the development's budget, without harming the financials, to make the project work and the hard cost pricing (cost of doing the building) is the largest needle mover.

Design Managers & Construction Managers:

Constructability is an important part of a project, after all why would you design something that can't be built. That is where the construction managers and the general contractor come into play. Construction Managers and General Contractors have vast experience in the construction world, and they have insights into designs that might not be readily available to the design team, especially if building in a new market. Some of the insights that can come from having an early interaction with the local players is the typical material selections in the area (higher vs. lower cost materials), typical building frame structure (wood vs light gauge), typical subterranean conditions in the area, and typical waterproofing best practices (waterproofing the slabs, basement walls). All of these are just the tip of the iceberg when it comes to the value of having a construction-oriented team on board early on.

Design Managers & Third-Party Design Consultants:

In addition to managing the aesthetics of a building to please the city as well as managing the design to assure its affordability, the design managers are in charge of making sure that the correct third-party design consultants are part of the project. There are multiple design consultants that need to be onboarded to support the project, some of them but not all, are mentioned below:

1. Structural
2. Structural Peer Reviewer
3. Landscape Architect
4. MEP Consultant
5. MEP Design Builder
6. LEED Consultant
7. Waterproofing Consultant
8. Low Voltage Consultant
9. Accessibility Consultant
10. Trash Consultant

All these consultants provide critical direction to the architect by providing them designs that already incorporate the codes and ordinances to make the project code compliant. The final step here is the architect taking their plans and coordinating all disciplines (i.e. making sure that all the electrical, mechanical, plumbing, and structural disciplines don't clash within the building).

Chapter 7:
Construction Management;
Boots on the Ground

Construction Management Team:

I think that it is safe to say that things are better when you have a group of people that you know have your back. In a way, that is what the owner's construction management group is assembled for. They are the group of individuals that will fight to safeguard the interests of the owner and assure that the projects are delivered on time and on budget at the desired quality of the developer.

As a developer, it is common to have an internal construction management group that will take care of the interests of the project from a budgetary, schedule, and quality perspective. The construction management team is typically composed of young individuals or seasoned professionals in the engineering, architectural, or construction management fields. Ideally the team is composed from a composite of all the fields mentioned above with experience ranges all over the time spectrum. In essence, this team is guiding and making the day-to-day decisions to inform the general contractor in its attempt to build the project on time and on budget. As a developer you should have clearly defined standards of what you expect to receive as a final product. Some of the standards that developers might have are the following:

1. Wall Finishes
2. Floor Finishes
3. Appliances
4. Fixtures
5. Signage
6. Cabinets

The construction management team will make sure to review submittals to assure that these meet the expectations and requirements for the project. Most of the time, the submittals will be routed through the general contractor's construction management system (typically Procore or plan grid) to the architect for review. Once the architect reviews and approves, this team will take one final look and make sure that the architect didn't miss anything.

Pay apps:

One of the crucial duties of this team is to review and approve pay apps for funding. This is an incredibly important task as proper execution of this duty assures that the general contractor receives payment on time. In turn, this allows the general contractor to distribute payment to its subcontractors for timely payment as well. Timely payments assure that the project continues proceeding forward smoothly towards completion. The project manager will review pay apps and make sure that the percentages billed for the project are a true reflection of the activities completed in the field. The general contractor will put together their pay application, which is composed of their subcontractors' pay applications, and they will review it with the developer's project manager to assure that the costs are accurate of the status of the project. Additionally, the construction manager engages in financial reporting for the job and trends the costs towards the end of the project to gauge whether the project is trending to be over budget, on budget, or under budget. This reporting usually gets shared with the executive team of the firm as well as with any consultants that capital partners, such as private equity firms or banks, have retained to keep an eye on the project.

Value Engineering & Budgets:

A critical role of the developer's construction manager is to manage budgets. As you know, budgets are set into stone at least 2 years before construction starts which means that costs in the market can change for the better or for the worse in the sense that they can make a budget obsolete or vice versa make it a healthy budget. In my experience it's typically the former rather than the latter, which means that construction managers are always working with general contractors to value engineer budgets to get them as close in line as possible. Value engineering is the process through which the general contractor and the owner's representative go through the project drawings and identify areas in which they can save money by using cost effective materials and construction processes, without sacrificing quality, to bring the project's budgets back in line. I have had the pleasure of working with very talented project managers as well as contractors. I have first-hand seen how they value engineer (value engineering is the process through which cheaper materials or designs are concocted without sacrificing value for the project) three hundred thousand dollars out of a design in order to bring the budget back in line, truly impressive.

Change Orders:

A change order is the legal contractual process through which money is added or deducted from a project. We previously spoke about the value engineering process. Once this process is completed during construction, the next step is documenting and changing the budgets. To do this, a change order encompassing all the changes in materials and the savings for each needs to be executed in order to formalize the changes. The same process is followed in case money needs to be added into the project. This typically happens when there are scope gaps in the drawings, extenuating market conditions impact the project, pandemics occur (too relatable), schedule acceleration is needed, or anything else that is not part of the original contract in between the owner and the general contractor is introduced into the project. Whenever a change order is issued by the general contractor, the construction manager is charged with reviewing all pricing documentation to make sure that the deductions from the budget are correct and that the additions are correct. As an owner, you always need to make sure that the general contractor is giving you back the full amount of the deduction and not adding more money than should be added to the budget if any additions are required.

Procurement / Buyout:

Timing in construction, like in many other fields, is of substantial importance. Hence a timely procurement of scope and subcontractors for the project will set up the project nicely for a smooth delivery. One of the key things to understand here is that both the long durations of construction projects and the uncertainty of the economy poses cost escalation and labor allocation risk. The cost escalation risk can be illustrated with a simple example. The general contractor will go into a contract with the developer to buy appliances for the job for a lump sum number of five hundred thousand dollars. Seems straightforward, except that months and months might go by in between the time that the contract is signed between the owner and contractor and the time in which the appliances are needed. This opens the general contractor to multiple risks. The longer the general contractor waits to buy the appliances, the more vulnerable he is to world changing factors that could impact the price such as for example, a war in Europe, a pandemic, and inflation. Hence, in order to assure the health of the promised budget, the contractor needs to procure and lock the appliances at an early stage in the construction process to lock in the price which will hopefully be the five hundred thousand dollars that was promised at the time of his contract with the owner/developer. It might also be the case that the general contractor is able to buy the appliances for a lower number, in which case there would be buyout savings. The use of buyout savings for a project needs to be clearly stipulated in the contract between the general contractor and the owner in order to avoid contention later down the line. The construction manager for the developer will take ownership of assuring that the general contractor is meeting the stipulated buy out dates for the multiple items for the project.

Schedules:

As you can probably guess, schedules are extremely useful in tracking the progress of your development. Tracking schedules will allow you as the developer to understand the health of your development from a timing standpoint. Timing of your development's delivery will dictate a large portion of your development's success. There are some industries in which the timing of a project delivery is much more crucial than in others. Typically, multifamily developments are not severely impacted if a project's schedule is somewhat delayed. It goes without saying that the goal of a project manager should be to mitigate delays and if one is incurred in the project, then the project manager should work to eliminate the delay and make up any lost time. The reason that multifamily projects are not typically substantially afflicted by a delay is because in the multifamily market, people are always moving in and out of states, regions, cities, and even within the city at different times during the year. Therefore, if a delivery is pushed, there is still a high likelihood that leases will be signed in advance of the opening as people plan their move to your building. In the student living world that is not the case. Within the student living world, one must deliver to the market the fall of the start of classes in order for students to have a place to live on campus once they begin their semesters.

It is very typical that as construction is ongoing, the property management team will commence to market the building concurrently and look to pursue the execution and signing of leases. For reasons you are thinking about already, this is a risk but one that must be taken to have a profitable development. In essence, the property management team is promising to the students that signed a lease that the building that's currently under construction, their apartment, will be delivered in time for their move in the fall. As a consequence of not delivering in time, a multitude of leases/tenants will not have a place to live once they try to move in. Developers have had this problem in the past and they typically go out of their way to accommodate all affected individuals in hotels and other apartments while their building is completed. This can be very expensive, a logistical nightmare, and reputationally destructive. Hence, it's paramount to manage the schedule so that the project doesn't get to that point. In most cases, projects will undergo in one shape or form, a delay to the project schedule. So what happens next? The only thing that can be done; accelerate. Acceleration of a schedule can be expensive but for the reason previously mentioned, it's worth it to spend the funds in the construction phase to deliver on time and keep your reputation as a developer in good standing and your tenants satisfied. Acceleration of a schedule requires a team effort during a time where conversations may turn less than amicable between the developer and the contractor; however, the developer and the contractor need to push the blame game aside and think about how they can work together to deliver the building on time. There are different strategies that developers and contractors use to accelerate projects. Some of the following can be found below:

1. Resequencing the critical path
2. Working overtime
3. Working Saturdays and Sundays
4. Procuring extra manpower
5. Rotating shifts
6. Pre-fabricating efficiencies

All of these options pose different challenges, most of which revolve around manpower. The construction industry is known for having labor shortages that have worsened through time and there is no telling if they will get any better in the foreseeable future. Thus even if the funds are available to pay for overtime and extra construction crews, if there is no labor the project won't be able to be accelerated. This is why having a competent general contractor that is well known in the locality where you are developing is important as they know the market and its subcontractors and have forged all those relationships which will aid in the efforts to push the project. One final note on schedules: when looking to accelerate a project, it's important to accelerate activities in the critical path. The critical path is the sequence of construction activities that dictate construction completion. The activities in this sequence are those that, if delayed 1 day, the project incurs a 1-day delay. Logically, those are the activities to be targeted for acceleration efforts. The same major activities are typically always in the critical path. These are the foundations, superstructure, dry-in, and MEPs. The first two are in the critical path for obvious reasons, but the latter may be a bit more cryptic if one does not have much construction experience. The dry-in is when the inside building will be all closed and protected from the elements. This is an important milestone as this is one of the precursors to start the installation of drywall and finishes. One does not want to start installing drywall without being completely dried in as this poses the risk of the drywall being damaged and consequences needing to strip it down and re-do all the work. The other aspect is the MEPs. MEPs stands for mechanical, electrical, and plumbing systems. MEPs that will be behind drywalled walls or ceilings need to be inspected prior to the full installation and drywalling of the walls and ceilings. If these are not inspected, drywalling and finishes won't be able to start. Some of these "critical" activities may differ slightly based on the nature of the asset that is to be delivered. As you see now, keeping track of activities is imperative and monthly issuance of updated schedules showing progress should be part of the project manager's requirements during the construction cycle.

Allowances & Contingencies:

Every project has what are called allowances and contingencies built into their project budgets. Allowances are basically buckets of money identified within the project for specific purposes. An example would be to say when there aren't any interior designs for the amenity spaces completed at the time of signing the contract with the general contractor. At this point, the contractor and you as the owner should anticipate that the construction of the interior amenity spaces will still need to be built. In this case the general contractor and the owner need to come to an agreement as to how much money to allocate for the construction of these specific spaces. This is typically informed by the general contractor's as well as the developer's experience on a per square footage basis. Contingencies are similar but not the same. Contingencies are not budgeted for a predetermined case. It is a budget that's placed into the project for any items that couldn't be reasonably anticipated. There are multiple examples of events that would resonate with the definition above such as a pandemic, a world war, hurricane, flood, etc. There are some examples that steer away from the "acts of God " arena into a more technical position such as an omission within the design that carries out extra construction costs in the field, or another good one would be the acceleration of efforts of the schedule. It's important that there is clear language as to what the process is to use such funds within the agreement between the general contractor and the developer. Additionally, if there are any funds available at the end of the job it is important that a clear split in savings be defined early on and be memorialized in the contract.

Punching:

Let's talk a bit about punching. Punching is one of the last activities that occur in a construction project as the delivery dates begin to approach. The name is misleading as this is not the time in which people start punching each other (although this can sometimes happen towards the end of a job as stress is at its highest), but rather is the time in which the owner/developer walks the project with the general contractor to review the quality of the product the general contractor is planning on delivering. During this phase, the owner will point out all quality deficiencies to the contractor and let the contractor know what needs to be fixed. There's a story of how this process ended up being called "punch". The legend goes that in the past, when owners/developers saw deficiencies in the craftsmanship of the general contractor, say a smudge on the wall, the owner/developer would "punch" the wall and make a hole in it to make sure that the general contractor fixed it. This is not something that happens on projects (I say that tongue in cheek because tempers fly and it can happen) and it's important to be realistic as to what level of quality was bought for the project as this process, if turned combative, could strain the relationship with the general contractor.

These are the few overarching things that the owner's/developer's construction management team handles as there are a multiple of issues that come about every day in construction projects, and it is extremely beneficial to have someone with previous experience to validate or invalidate the issues claimed by the general contractor from a cost or schedule standpoint. As mentioned before, the owner's/developer's team is the group of individuals that will be in the trenches to assure and fight for the owner's interests from the very beginning. As we have seen, construction projects are riddled with challenges that stem from procurement and scheduling to budget management. Furthermore, there are the issues that no project member is aware of as there are unanticipated problems that were inherently a part of the project. As you can understand at this point, with all the complexity and uncertainty inherent to a project, having a team of highly experienced and motivated individuals will be of great value to the project and a cost worth spending.

Chapter 8:
General Contractors;
The Builders

General Contracting Team:

We have discussed quite a bit about the different disciplines and players involved in creating a project on paper. It is now time to discuss the next step: taking all the prints and designs and turning it into a tangible real thing, a building. We have previously mentioned how the different teams are involved at a very preliminary level with general contractors. As you recall, the general contractor tends to be involved in some capacity when the drawings are being developed to provide pricing information as well as constructability reviews. Well, at some point the drawings need to be turned into an actual building to complete the development. This is done through extensive negotiations between the general contractor and the ownership group (developer). The General Contractor is a builder in the city where the development will be situated. General contractors have the experience of the various idiosyncrasies of building projects on their "turf" which is useful when one is trying to understand pricing and schedule durations for construction purposes.

General Contractors & Subcontractors:

General contractors need to have serious & healthy relationships with the various sub-contractors in the area. These relationships enable contractors to have a team of specialty builders under their team in order to build the project on time, on budget, and within the specified level of quality required by the owner. Some of this specialty subs or subcontractors are the following:

1. Civil Contractor

2. Mechanical Contractor
3. Electrical Contractor
4. Plumbing Contractor
5. Concrete Contractor

These contractors will make or break the development and having a general contractor that vouches for them due to their experience working with them provides a level of comfort to the developer. Aside from using the local contractor for their experience with qualified contractors, they should be used to receive the best pricing (this is sometimes called preferential pricing). Let me explain. The best pricing is provided by the subcontractors to the general contractor that they have worked with before and liked, essentially a contractor they trust. In a way, subcontractors can indirectly sway the developer's decision on who to go with as the general contractor as they can provide astronomically high numbers for their work to a general contractor they don't know as well as provide exceptionally competitive pricing to the general contractor they do know.

General Contractors & City Building Departments:

Furthermore, a local contractor should have access to relationships with the city. I would be weary of a contractor that has worked in a certain city and has failed to foster positive relationships with the city. The city's perception of the general contractor is incredibly important. When the city trusts a general contractor, they are willing to accommodate the project's needs in a much more organic way. Sometimes, there will be times where an emergency inspection will need to be conducted by the city's inspector in order to keep the project on schedule and if the contractor doesn't have the political capital to ask for an expedited inspection, then the chances are that the inspection won't happen. On the other hand, if the contractor has worked with the inspector before and they have a longstanding relationship, it is very likely that the inspection will occur.

A good contractor has political capital with the city they work with. One example of the benefit of having a general contractor with amicable relationships with the city is at the time of closing out the project and achieving the certificate of occupancy (CofO). The certificate of occupancy is the final document that the city gives the general contractor certifying that the building is ready for people to live in it. As you can imagine this is a huge milestone for the overall project team because this means that tenants can move into their respective apartments or offices or whatever the space might be; which in turn means cash inflow for the developer in the form of rents paid. However, it is not always smooth sailing. There are times when the project might be delayed during construction and the full building, meaning residential units plus common areas and amenities, is not complete. At this point the general contractor along with the owner need to go over to the city and ask to see if a temporary certificate of occupancy can be obtained. A temporary certificate of occupancy is a certification which basically states that tenants can move into the building contingent on the prohibited use of unfinished areas and many other stipulations that the city might want to incorporate into the temporary certificate of occupancy (TCO). As you can see, this is a big ask from the project team as it is one that requires that the city trusts the team to assure that all contingencies are in place and that the remaining work to officially fully close out the building still occurs in a timely manner. This is where the general contractor's political capital comes into play. The city will be more amenable to the idea of issuing a temporary certificate of occupancy if they have done so in the past to the same general contractor on your project and if they delivered and kept their promise. If the city has had a negative experience with the general contractor in your project, chances are a TCO won't be issued.

General Contractors & Document Management:

One intrinsic role to the general contractor is the responsibility of documenting the construction of the project from an architectural, engineering, and financial perspective. There are multiple document management software's in the industry which are widely employed by general contractors but the ones that I have seen being used the most are Procore and PlanGrid. Both of these are very similar and serve the same purpose; documentation. I previously alluded in the book to the use of RFIs and submittals. The general contractor will use Procore and PlanGrid to document and communicate project information. A submittal, as it was previously mentioned, is the package that documents the type of materials and all relevant information about the products being used to build the project. The project's submittals will get uploaded and transferred to the different reviewers. As each reviewer reviews the submittal, they will approve it and will pass it on to the next reviewer. This process will continue until it goes through all the reviewers and it gets the approved "seal" for formal documentation.

As previously mentioned, an RFI is a "Request for Information." A request for information is when the general contractor has an open-ended question about how the project is to be built. It is worth mentioning that the architect makes an incredible attempt to have all the plans and specs laid out to build the project, but sometimes there are things that don't get spelled out very detailed or there might be two contradicting notes in the plan, so on and so forth. In order to document the direction that the general contractor was provided, the general contractor will upload the RFI to the software for document management (Procore or PlanGrid) and will route it to the architect. In turn, the architect will review the RFI and if the question is for him then he will answer the question. Some other times, the question might be geared towards the structural engineer or the civil engineer. In that case, the architect will forward the question and will make sure that it gets answered. Once the RFI is answered the architect will return the RFI and will mark it as "answered". From there on, the general contractor will take the RFI and use it to continue building the project and it will be documented.

General Contractors & As-Built Drawings:

After all the required submittals have been documented and all the RFIs have been answered the contractor will document how the project was actually built compared to the construction drawings, submittals, and RFIs. The general contractor does that along with the architect very simply by taking the original drawings and marking them up and referencing the different RFIs with any clarifying drawings that document the actual built condition. At the end of the project the as-built conditions are turned over to the owner/developer.

General Contractors & Project Financials:

Another element that the contractor is responsible for is reporting of the financial health of the project. Contractors use a financial document called AIA G701 and AIA G702 in which the different sub-contract values (budgets for the different scopes of work: steel, masonry, earthwork, etc.) are listed. As the project progresses the budgets start to change and dwindle, some contract values will increase and some will dwindle. All of this needs to get documented and tracked. Understanding where all the money is going and if anything got reallocated within the budget is critical for the financial management of a project. As previously mentioned, there are different legal instruments to change budgets and have them be officially part of the project. This is the change order process through which the use of the allowance and contingency budgets are accessed. This document not only shows the original contract values, but also the percentage complete, percentage remaining, and new contract values. This document gets compiled once a month and gets submitted to the owner/developer for payment approval, so on and so forth, until the project is closed out.

General Contractors & Closeout:

When the project reaches completion, the general contractor needs to take all the documentation from the project such as submittals, RFIs, As-Builts, etc. and turn it over to the owner. It is important that the ownership group/developer review all the documentation. One of the crucial pieces of documentation are the warranties for the project. Warranties are the documents that provide anything in between a year or two of, let's call it "insurance" coverage, to the building systems. It's crucial to verify that these are in place because building systems can fail or have quality issues with them due to the installation methods that were used or just faulty fabrication of the material in the product that was installed. The warranty is the assurance from the installer that they will come back to fix it, free of charge, as long as the request is within the time frame of the warranty. This item is the most important for the property management and leasing team, which we will talk about next.

Chapter 9:
Property Managers & Leases; The Salesman

Property Management Team:

A good way to think of the property management and leasing team is to think of them as the salesman of the product, the rental property. The property management team will be composed of the people that are in charge of marketing the project as the newest and greatest apartment (or whatever other asset type is being marketed) on the block. As you can see the function of this team is a big deal as a rental property that is not rented/leased is a massive failure. Since developers cannot afford to have a vacant property, they dedicate resources, financial or otherwise, to a property management and leasing team. Aside from leasing the property (we will talk about lease types in a second) the property management team is tasked with managing the daily operations of the property. This means that this team is in charge of making sure rents are paid, walking prospective tenants around the property, assuring maintenance requests are fulfilled, maintaining amenities in good quality, and anything else that may come up related to the operations of the building. As promised, let's discuss leases.

Property Management & Leases:

There are multiple types of leases that are used to bring a prospective tenant under a legal obligation to pay for the use of the asset built. A couple of the most common ones in the space are triple net leases (NNN), full-service leases (FS), and modified gross leases (MG). Triple net leases are those in which the tenant pays for all expenses, this type of lease is very common for commercial properties, and it entails that the tenant will end up paying for all expenses such as taxes, insurance, maintenance, etc. The responsibility of payments by the tenant typically depends on a proportion of the tenant's occupied space. When the tenant ends up sharing the responsibility for covering a percentage or all the expenses on a property, the base rent will be lower. Thus, properties that use net type leases have lower base rents than other types of leases. Full-service leases are the opposite of triple net leases in the sense that the tenant does not pay for any of the expenses. Thus, base rents are the highest. Modified gross leases are somewhat of a hybrid in between triple net and full-service leases, meaning that the tenant can be responsible for some expenses but not all of them. Thus, base rents are typically somewhere in between full service and triple net leases. The type of lease that will be used in the development is important to consider from the very beginning as this has an impact on how expenses are being paid for within the development. The lease type should be discussed at the beginning of the project in between the investments team and the property management team as this will have an impact on the financial modeling aspect of the project. Another aspect to consider about leases is the time that they will remain effective. There are pros and cons to long period leases and short period leases. To illustrate the variability of lease length, we can think about a hotel. Hotels have lease lengths of nights. When you pay a hotel to stay a night or a week, you are essentially signing a lease. In the case of hotels, this would be considered short term leases. The con is that the property management team needs to constantly source tenants. The advantage is that rates can be adjusted on a daily basis. In comparison, industrial properties might have lease lengths of five years or more. With long term leases, it might be difficult to increase rent rates. A provision may be included in the lease that allows ownership to increase rents, but that will probably be negotiated with the prospective tenant. The important idea to take from this is that leases drive cash flow into the property and cash is king.

Property Management & Operations/Maintenance:

Aside from making sure that the property is leased to bring in tenants into the building, the property management team needs to make sure that the building runs smoothly. When a new building opens, it is a fact that there will be kinks around the building and the property management team will have to be present to solve those issues. Typical issues that occur within a couple of weeks of move-in might be, but are not limited to: fixing air conditioning systems in the units, replacing appliances, and replacing flooring. Whenever any of the aforementioned issues pops up, the tenants need to communicate it to the property managers. When it comes to buildings with a large number of units and tenants, it is fairly practical to have some sort of portal where residents can submit a work order for the deficiency to be fixed. This is where having a maintenance team becomes crucial. The property management team needs to make sure to have a maintenance team of one or more than one person in order to address all the issues that spring up around the building. Another reason for which a building maintenance team is important is for the rest of the miscellaneous tasks to be managed around the property. Some of these include but are not limited to the following below:

- Landscaping (maintaining any green areas in a healthy condition)

- Trash management (making sure the trash is where it needs to for pick up)
- Snow management (making sure that the roads are salted, and any excess snow is removed)
- Fire alarm testing (making sure all emergency systems are running smoothly)
- Elevator maintenance (making sure elevators are in good stance to operate)
- Work order fulfillment (making sure work orders are closed out)
- Pool cleaning (making sure pools are clean)
- Fitness maintenance (making sure equipment is clean and faulty equipment is repaired)

All of these are by no means an all-inclusive list but they provide a good idea as to why a maintenance team is important.

Chapter 10:
Thinking Forward

Thinking about what real estate might look like in the future can be a daunting task, but I think it's safe to say that available prime real estate will dwindle as time passes by. After all, as the old adage goes, "Buy land because God isn't making any more of it." This means that there will be a force of expansion forcing cities to grow either away from their downtown centers, even more than they are now, or pressures to build vertically and be even more efficient with available land. Additionally, I believe that there will be an increase in land re-positioning. What I mean by this is that there will be an increase in trade of existing properties with buildings already on them. This entails that new real estate deals will have to be either programmed for the existing asset to be repositioned in the market i.e., turning a mall into an apartment complex or completely demolishing the existing structure to make way for another use of the land. Additionally, I think that the age of having environmentally clean properties is coming to a close. It is the case that, more and more, developments will have to deal with remediating a property.

I believe that this is a good thing as this involves the remediation and cleanup of impacted soils and groundwater that could inadvertently affect communities. Furthermore, I expect that there will be a great shift into property technology. There are already multiple firms leading this effort, but tech companies have really been absent from servicing the built environment. I imagine that this will change, and buildings will have integrated systems that will shape the living dynamic experience for renters and other stakeholders. For example, I estimate that the use of keys to get in and out of apartments will become obsolete. I still believe that keys will be used but I reckon that the use of electronic means of accessing units, amenities, and just access across the building will trend towards digital keys. System integrations and partnerships such as Amazon, Apple, and Uber will become a thing. Buildings are already adapting to the increase of waste generated by amazon packages as well as incorporating into them specific areas for ride sharing. More of this will become the norm.

Sustainability concerns will more than likely become a leading item of discussion on the investments side as well as on the jurisdictional side. California, for example, has already started to eliminate the use of gas within new construction buildings. All buildings within specific cities like San Francisco and Berkeley have already banned the use of natural gas in an effort to diminish the use of fracking. I personally don't believe this will be a national or world standard, but I do believe there will be some wide adoption within different areas of the United States and maybe in different countries. I do think, however, that this adoption can only be afforded by affluent countries within the developed world and not by developing countries.

Within the construction industry, there is a large initiative to pivot the construction process to much more of a manufacturing process. There are initiatives out there where buildings are being prefabricated and brought out into pieces and assembled onsite. Construction companies are starting to realize that there is a schedule and quality benefit from manufacturing different building systems on a fabrication shop somewhere else and then bringing them into the jobsite for installation. I think that this trend will take over as time passes by. However, I don't think that a fully pre-manufactured building, if you will, is going to become a norm. The reason being is that there are many different codes and regulations that vary at multiple levels of analysis; they vary from building type to building type, city to city, state to state, and country to country. Due to this variability, having a fully manufactured process is virtually impossible. In order to have a truly manufactured system, one must standardize the product first, so that the production process is the same for every unit, and then lay out the line of production. In construction, the standardization of the "unit" is not possible as every site has different constraints that force designers to pursue different solutions. However, I do think that specific elements of a building will continue to be prefabricated. Some of the systems that I see being predominantly prefabricated are the following:

- Electrical Panels
- Plumbing Runs
- Interior Wall Assemblies
- Concrete

Additionally, I think that buildings will stop being operated as siloed structures but rather they will become incorporated into a network of buildings to provide value to the client. Let me explain. In order for a tenant to rent a space within the building, the tenant needs to sign a lease. Leases can be seen as "handcuffs" by tenants as they eliminate flexibility to move around to other apartments if they wish to do so. This can be detrimental to the tenant as life is full of uncertainty and maybe the tenant finds a new job in another city or needs to move out for personal reasons prior to the end of the executed lease agreement. I surmise that to provide greater value to tenants, developers will start to realize that they can benefit from network effects. Network effects are the phenomenon in which the value of a service or good depends on the number of users of the service or good. For example, cell phones. Cellphones are not very useful if only one person has a cellphone. In order for a cellphone to be valuable, more than one person needs to have a cell phone and those cell phones need to be able to interact with each other. I consider this same idea applies to real estate. I think that developers will commence to make sure that every building they develop will be part of a wider network of buildings which will be open to their tenants. Leases will become flexible and allow tenants to seamlessly move across different buildings as they need to. The more buildings that are part of the network the more valuable the network will be to the potential tenant. For example, say a developer has developed and acquired 50 buildings across different cities within the United States and as part of its service, it provides flexible leases to its clients. Say maybe their lease allows them to use any of the 50 buildings, provided there is room available, across the country. I expect that this is the next step for the real estate industry.

I hope that you have found this book instructive and insightful as you begin your journey within the exciting world of real estate. With that I leave you, after all…we are all…always in a hurry!

www.ingramcontent.com/pod-product-compliance
Lightning Source LLC
Chambersburg PA
CBHW070259220526
45465CB00004B/1666